THE LAST WALTZ

Also by D.M.Thomas:

novels
The Flute-Player
Birthstone
The White Hotel
Russian Nights Quintet:
  Ararat
  Swallow
  Sphinx
  Summit
  Lying Together
Flying in to Love
Pictures at an Exhibition
Eating Pavlova
Lady with a Laptop
Charlotte
Hunters in the Snow

verse novels
Vintage Ghosts
Corona Man

verse memoir
A Child of Love and War

poetry
Penguin Modern Poets 11
Two Voices
Logan Stone
Love and Other Deaths
The Honeymoon Voyage
Dreaming in Bronze
The Puberty Tree: *Selected Poems*
Dear Shadows
Not Saying Everything
Unknown Shores: *Collected SF poems*
Shadow Sonnets
Flight and Smoke
Two Countries
Mrs English and Other Women
Family Bible

translations
Akhmatova: *Selected Poems*
Pushkin: *Selected Poems*
Onegin
Ruslan and Ludmila
Yevtushenko: *A Dove in Santiago*

memoirs
Memories & Hallucinations
Bleak Hotel

biography
Alexander Solzhenitsyn: *a Century in his Life*
Coffee with Freud

stageplay
Hell Fire Corner

children's fiction
The Devil and the Floral Dance

See also dmthomasonline.net

THE LAST WALTZ

Poems

D.M. THOMAS

The Cornovia Press
SHEFFIELD

Published by The Cornovia Press, Sheffield, 2021

ISBN 978 1 908878 22 9

Contents

One

Two

One

Eye

(*sestina*)

It's no fun being a hypochondriac. Take my eye
That was recently operated on, the right.
It always had far sight, yet was weak
Compared with the left, with which I've read
Without glasses always; called 'lazy' or 'sleepy',
It's the master eye. They've both suffered wear and tear

From too many sad sights, inconsolable tears.
But, mercifully almost, it's simply my right eye
I'm aware of, all other griefs and worries sleep.
Find a distraction, my wife says: write!
I try. My hand shakes, for that distant red
Roof seems, surely, a shade dimmer than last week?

I strain to reach my dropped e-cig; two weeks
After surgery can the tiny incision still tear
From straining? For me, yes. The eye will grow red,
Angry; an infection in my right eye
Could blind! One in a thousand, but that's me—right?
I'm certain it is happening in my sleep,

Though the fear, of course, curtails my sleeping.
I open that eye often, to check if the vision is weaker:
'A rapid visual loss…' Christ! No, it's alright.
I think. The cataract op, from the first careful tear
In the cornea, went well, the lights my zonked eye
Could see mesmeric, the surgeon well-read,

Urbane, jokey. By the next morning I saw reds,
Greens, yellows, in far-off vistas that had slept
For many years. It felt miraculous; I
Was reborn. Ah yes, but four weeks
Of eye drops, stinging as if the eye were torn
Apart or branded in some malign demonic rite!

And my left eye looks larger than the right
In the mirror. Admittedly there's no redness,
But it could become too small to shed a tear.
I dare not hope; for when anxiety briefly sleeps
Fate strikes. Dear God of light, why am I so weak?
My *I* has shrunk, like my right eye,

Until now it is entirely in my right eye;
It is that eye, not my pen, that is writing;
At night it is a Red Giant star, by my wife asleep.

The Madman

'Dear God, let me not go mad,'
Wrote Pushkin. Amen to that.
There were no drugs to cure it in his day.
You might say, nor today. But we can dull it
With antipsychotics, or with lithium.

Yet there's one form of madness nothing helps,
The madness of being in love.
It takes one over unstoppably, like a deadly virus.
I suffered from that once, and did not know it,
Thought I was happy, though giving others pain.
I followed her around the world.
I should have been trussed up in a straitjacket.

I almost lost my soul. Thank God in time
My sanity came back. I glanced at photos,
Kept in a secret place, removed furtively
To sigh over, and suddenly realised
They were just pictures of an ordinary
Woman, her face attractive in a round

Placid way. All women are cows, horses
Or cats. I was made for cat women.
I wouldn't need to look at these photos again.
It was an immense release. I had been
Not in my right mind. My Fool, brother to
King Lear's, leapt onto my lap and said,
'I've been trying to tell you that, nuncle.'

The Call

It is a mild evening. Darkness has fallen.
I am waiting patiently near a phone box.
A man is making a call, another
waits outside, and not wishing to crowd him
I stand a couple of paces to the side.

Quite suddenly four or five other people
approach from along the pavement
heading for the phone box. Quickly I
move in ahead of them to stand
just behind the man at the head of
what is now a queue.

He enters the vacated box,
and I move up close.
I start to wonder what I shall talk about
with my wife. I feel slightly anxious.
There is that bit of good news about
my novel, but I think I may have
told her that during our last phone call.
In any case it's not enough.

A door bangs shut from a sudden
gust of wind, waking me from
my light afternoon sleep. My eyes open
to bright sunlight in our bedroom. I feel
a stab of sorrow for I was so close to
hearing her voice again,
still familiar and loved
though she died twenty years ago,
but mixed with it is
relief
for I have always been terrible
at phone calls, halting, barely articulate.

Still I can't believe in her death,
and if our talk had gone badly
I'd have felt awful
walking away from the phone box.

God at Godrevy

(*i.m. Jessica Thomas*)

Too crammed in the back corner to remove
My jacket in the June heat, yet
Broiling I rushed here! … Christ, there's not a hymn
To stand up for, and no relief
In ritual, everything, as she would wish, dry.
I'll burn alive… 'I'm going to faint,' I lie
To my wife. Others may think it's grief
—Which is curiously absent, though I love

The woman in the wicker casket—that sends
Me crashing over court shoes
And slingbacks, while her aged sister's voice
Starts frailly, and all are turning
Their heads at the ruckus behind, but I'm free,
Tumbling into the arms of the funeral guy!
I imagine the silenced author yearning
To turn this drollery to her creative ends,

Fictive ideas surging, at night, late.
Now I can think of her
With a calm mind, while sipping shakily
From a paper cup. Widowed, removed

From Cornwall to London, how strangely she
Was taken, back briefly, gazing out to sea
At the Godrevy Light, so loved
By her and Charles, no longer separate.

Dear friend, I rushed, fearing your maimèd rites,
To sit where I'd have to flee.
Yes, God may not exist, but I'm not equal
To that, preferring to think there's One
Who—like us in our small way—invents endlessly.
Mother and daughter, planning to go for tea…
Instead you died, foreseeing a sequel.
I think you glimpsed, beyond the Light, more lights.

The School Walk

(*i.m. Linda Laidman*)

The storm outside is echoing in my head
With grief for you, and thought of your long pain.
Sixty years back we shared the hill that led
To Teignmouth Grammar from the Dawlish train.
I don't recall the humdrum things we said
Those morning walks, but do recall our ease,
Pupil and new young teacher, our common tread.

And then, in lessons, how you loved to tease!
Taking their mock A-levels my whole class
Misquoted 'we pissed along the polished ice'
Instead of 'hissed…'—put up to it by you,
Knowing I'd love the joke, and all would pass!
Lurking, the flame of beauty I later knew,
But rainy mornings lightened, so bright your face.

A Late Dream

(*i.m. Ray Embleton*)

I have never dreamed of him before,
My sister's husband, in age
Too remote to call him my brother-in-law,
Short and bumptious, back in '49
When we shared their Melbourne flat;
His daughter says, 'If you asked dad the time
He would tell you the history of clocks.'

When Lois exercised on the lounge floor
He flew into a sudden rage,
Seeing me ogle what we all saw
For I was directly in line
With her wheeling thighs, nyloned, fat;
An erection was hardly a crime,
But he shoved me back in my box.

I knew he'd flown in the war
But all he had done was off-stage,
The bombing raids when he would draw
The flightpath to Hamburg or Köln;
I'd no conception of that,
A boy excited by war, seeing flame

Light the night sky over Falmouth docks.

He should have perished long before
His twenty fifth, last mission in a cage
Being blown around like a straw
Once they'd droned over the Rhine,
While I was linseed-oiling my bat
For the next day's cricket game
On our croft, all furze and rocks:

For few survived, and he knew the score;
But at twenty, alive still, turned the page
To his first kiss, first unhooked bra,
Marriage—then the constant whine
Of a homesick, know-all, English brat,
Who listened for sex when he came
Creeping past at night like a fox.

Lois, a carefully nurtured flower,
Had landed homesick, couldn't engage
With his family, hard-living and raw.
Ray loved her staunchly, didn't repine,
Toiled to give her the comfort she sought.
At fifty, his heart weak, the Reaper's aim

Was sharper than Hitler's swastika'd hawks.

Now at last, at eighty four,
I'm extolling him from a dream-stage,
As a brave, with the odd flaw,
But his virtues far greater than mine.
It's late to be aiming at
Redress, but rising they roar his name,
This crowd in tuxedos and long frocks.

Shades

'Donald Thomas…' Christ! a chill runs through me;
Its tone is less a greeting than a threat.
I know that voice from sixty years ago,
Whipping me home from school: *'C'mon! Too slow!'*
I'm hobbling to the rugby stand, the weather gloomy,
The bank behind the goalposts slippery, wet.
He's growled my name from a trio of pensioners.
I croak out his in reply.

A cross between Larwood and a lunatic,
Demon-eyed, from a long run-up, he uncoiled
Our concrete cricket ball to smash our stick-
Stumps or my lovingly linseed-oiled,
Moon-cratered bat on our pitch of rocks and furze;
Tall, strong, all bony elbows and knees,
His face like a young Clint Eastwood's, lean and mean.
He had no mum. His house was arid and cold.
I was glad to put between us oceans and seas.

He sent me each month for a year carefully-rolled
And wrappered comics, thirteen thousand miles
To Melbourne. By then I was reading *Macbeth*

Not the Beano. He looks small now, with a stoop;
'Good cricketer,' he drawls to his chums, and smiles
At me, soft-faced; but he still scares me to death,
There's surely an irony in his smile and drawl,
They're no softer than that concrete ball.
I can hear *'C'mon! Too slow!'* feel the sting
Of his stick in between the whip-on of his hoop
Up Trewirgie Road. 'You blocked everything!'

I raise my walking-stick in a final
Salute then stumble on, as a drizzling rain
Moves in over Carn Brea. I should have said
Thanks for those comics. Never even paid
For the postage. Guilt, as I use a urinal
In the leaking, piss-stinking shack near the stand.
'You blocked everything.' What did he mean?
It sounded quite profound, not just the judder
Surging from bat-handle to shoulder
On that patch of granite-bouldered ground.

Epiphanies

September 1940: I tugging back
On mummy's hand, rain drizzling face and mac,
A gas mask box hung from around my neck.

The school, high, granite, grim as Colditz castle;
Into a mini-Auschwitz of partings, the bustle
Of a dank cloakroom, reeking toilets, rustle

Of tiny macs removed. Mummy eased my pain
Slightly with 'In no time you'll be home,' but then
Ruined it: 'No dear, you'll have to go again

Tomorrow.' And endless days away from home,
From our Cornish Range, the chirks still warm
To dress by, helped by my plump warm mum.

Then my tears slowed: a girl was standing near
Beside her mother, both with a calm air;
A pretty girl, with short straight flaxen hair;

She hinted, even at five, I might not bother
One far off day to cling on to my mother…

Then girls were led one way, we boys the other.

My memory of that infant would never go.
My briefest love affair? The first of two;
In dog days heat, the Melbourne sky burnt blue,

I sweating, burdened, on my way from school
To home, saw a girl green-blazered, cool,
At the tram stop. Her face was beautiful,

My age, mid-teens, with short straight flaxen hair;
I stood and gazed; her skin looked English, fair;
She gazed ahead, as if I were not there.

There was no traffic flowing in the street,
Silence embraced us in the sultry heat,
The cosmos stilled into a steady state.

Then her tram came; not mine. It was as brief,
That love affair—I could find no relief
From aching, hopeless longing; I still grieve.

Were they the same girl I saw twice?
For many sailed to find the Southern Cross;

Unlikely, but the same pure love and loss,

A joy gone as soon as seen, like rays
Of bright sun in a series of storm-black days
Which say, be thankful for such radiances.

Stella australis

I'd been 'Thomas' at my English Grammar School
To dim, starchy masters, and felt less than human;
When my first Aussie teacher—wondrously a woman—
Pretty, with short curly black hair, Scottish-cool

On a hot Melbourne day, asked me my name
I said Thomas. 'Can I call you Tom?' she asked.
Within moments I was 'Don' to her, and I basked
In that friendliness, felt lighter, bearing the same

Name as my hero Don Bradman. I caused alarm
In my family later, saying, 'Don't call me Donald,
I'm Don.' They never learned, but my life was channelled
In a different direction; Don is who I am.

One day she asked me to wait behind
After class, then with a gentle touch
On my arm, her eyes kind, she said, 'Don't slouch;
Don, you're a good-looking boy, but stand up straight.'

I bless you, Miss Gordon, wherever you are.
You cared about that slouching, stout, shy English boy;

Gazing at you I even learned to enjoy
Latin. Old, I can't stand up straight any more,

But I did for ages after your difficult intervention,
For it can't have been easy, embarrassing me
For my good. I want to say, *te amavi*,
I loved you. I wish you'd kept me in detention,

One whole hot hour of your lustrous ebony curls,
With all the other boys insanely jealous,
As after I write out a hundred lines of Catullus
You sit by me, and ask what I know about girls.

A Cornish Postcard

The up-train's smoke; families crowd the railings
For a last look at the miners dense below,
Bound for the Rand: 'The weekly Exodus
From Redruth station.' Cloth caps, Edwardian dress,
But Biblical the fervour cleaving through
Hard rock, as one by one the mines were failing.
Impromptu choirs, each week, to ease their pain
Sang *'God be with you till we meet again'.*

Shafts yawned beneath them as they poured out soul;
Rand drills were 'widow-makers'; letters took weeks,
Child-fevers less; and they might only meet,
Except through laboured words, *'at Jesus' feet'.*
The train will chug off, gather speed, heartaches
Will hide, among the men, glide into droll
Jibes at the Camborne dolts who swarmed aboard
A stop before; and the first grog is poured.

Their families will disperse, and plod their way
To poor streets or rough, grimy villages
Amidst the silent headgear all around.
I love these people, long now underground.

They are my tribe, at home or overseas.
I envy them their camaraderie;
I a grass captain who can only write
And *a capella* sing, 'Lead, kindly Light'.

The down-train platform, bare in the postcard's scene,
Is haunted by the memories of my father
Hunched in his old coat, awaiting my night-train
From Oxford. Love's greetings then were plain:
A firm handshake; drive home. Amid the heather
And gorse lay the grey ruins, softened in.
I blent in too, glad, though aware my mind
Was mining elsewhere, farther than the Rand.

My heart was, and would go on being, there,
In that small, straggly village of those I loved,
Its people poor, but humorous and kind,
By one another and flickering faith sustained.
My chapel-going over, I was moved
Still as I faintly heard the choir's Lord's Prayer
In sweet harmony; still hear it as it steals
Across long-settled, richly loded fields.

Grass captain: mine leader working above ground
'Lead, kindly Light' was known as the miners' hymn

Gigs

I suppose it's not so very different:
Van Morrison and his band performing his music
To a great crowd at the Eden Project,
The immense clay pit become an attraction,
And John Wesley preaching in the amphitheatre
At Gwennap Pit to thousands of worshippers.
Van has his amplifiers, John had great acoustics;
The cries and arm wavings at Eden echo
The shouts of *Hallelujah!* and *Praise the Lord!*
At Gwennap. Van has his bowler hat,
John his richly flowing white hair.

At both, no doubt, someone fainted, overcome,
Carried off to murmurs of compassion.

I can hear John's voice in 'But the healing, the HEALING,
Has begun!' Both crowds stream away uplifted
And dying for a piss. We're still only human,
We are all 'going down to the end of the land'.

When Van sings 'I want you to put on your pretty summer dress…
And all the rest', we must use our imaginations,

Just as John's had to, following his gaze skywards,
Calling on 'dear Lord Jesus'. Behold the man! Van the Van!

Only, at Gwennap, the congregation sang the hymns
In Cornish harmony, and they knew the rich cadences
Of the King James, even if most
Could not read; for below them and in them
Were deep productive mines still.
We have the net's omniscience and its cloud,
The cadences of *Fifty Shades of Grey*,
Wellness books, and tweets,
And no mines to go down in, level after level,
On the man engine.

Hats

(*sestina*)

Sterile days, nothing creative in my aged head,
The Muse's silence saying I've had my time.
I post on the virtual group to which I belong,
Our scattered family's roadhouse, 'Help, I'm blocked!
Give me a theme.' My reclusive younger son
In Peru instantly responds with 'Hats'.

No sooner do I think, 'What the fuck—*hats!*'
Than I see, perched on my dad's auburn-wavy head
The flat cap protecting him from rain or sun
And defining what he was in that class-ridden time,
Far on in his fifties heaving concrete blocks.
Yet anyone could see he didn't belong

There truly. He'd worn that cap for too long,
Mum scolded, and went with him to buy a trilby hat.
In her mind they were again living on the same block
As Dorothy Parker, both young, beautiful, ahead
Infinite possibilities in that Los Angeles springtime,
Golden among orange groves, under unending sun,

Mingling on film sets with the likes of Gloria Swanson;
And though he was only a workman, they belonged
Classlessly. Now, thirty years on, for a time
He looked proud again, a gent in his trilby hat,
'Jack as good as his master', holding his head
High. He marched with a sovereign tread, like Blok's

Twelve Red rebels following Christ. But the block
Was too great, sadness, like an eclipse of the sun,
Stole over him; the dreams in his head
Stayed hidden and unfulfilled. Among them he longed,
I believe, for passion. Face obscured by his hat,
He took a comely friend to the pictures for a time.

I don't think mum minded; she had no time
For the movie dramas he loved. Then a new block,
In his urinary tract. What happened to his trilby hat?
His new Burton's overcoat fitted his son,
The only thing I took from his belongings.
It was icy at his funeral, hail scalding my naked head.

He was crushed to death by the mountain of blocks
He had lifted, laid. I see him, shy in his new hat,
Alive, kind. It's only been fifty eight years: no time.

June Heat

A summer, almost fifty years ago.
My mistress, a young teacher, lived in a flat
High in a dark, redbrick Victorian house
In dour countryside. After her day stretching
Eight year old minds she'd come home, sticky, hot,
Climb gloomy flights of stairs. On reaching
Her bedroom she would peel off skirt and blouse,
Lie on her bed, just a sheet over her,
Close her eyes and half-drowse.

There was a black lad, aged fifteen or so,
Only son of the mixed race owners,
Who'd hover, chat. He had a boyish charm
And a clear crush on her—no shrivelled schoolma'am
But stylish, a looker, with an older lover.
She told me she sensed he sometimes came
Into her flat in her absence, using the key
His mother had. We guessed he would explore
Drawers, her always black stockings and underwear.

One afternoon, while resting on her bed,
She heard a key grate in the front door lock.

She froze. Knew it was him. Affected sleep.
She sensed there was no harm in him, she said.
But then she felt the thin sheet on her rise
And the boy's nervous, gentle touch
Over the stockings to her soft-fleshed thighs.
She went on breathing quietly, with closed eyes.
With the same silent footsteps he was gone.

This was the graceful boy, good at football,
I later saw in their garden jink and swerve,
Alone. She told me about that afternoon;
We were both outraged and admired his nerve:
She only had to scream, his mum would run
Up the stairs. The same happened the next day:
She lay, as if asleep, he came, he touched
With a moth's softness, swiftly crept away.
Beyond her thighs he had not dared to stray.

There was an element, in the oppressive
Languor, silence all around,
The woman wondrous under the thin sheet,
Tired and solitary, the boy obsessive,
Of myth and legend, princess in the tower;
He, black, shunned she guessed at his school,

So worshipful of her female power,
And she, so admirably cool…
If only I, at fifteen, had walked in his shoes!

On the third day, devilry made her choose
To overwhelm. I empathised his shock,
His turbulence, at that dark shrine revealed,
Framed by her taut suspender belt.
Unbearable tension. I imagined it.
His breathing changed and he was scared, she felt.
'The bugger had a finger in!' she chuckled.
Just for a moment, then the sheet fell back.
On the fourth day she changed the lock.

The question today, in our puritan house
Bleaker than Dickens', would be who abused whom?
It was anarchic Eros. In his old age
His life's book, I'm sure, opens at that page
Always, obsessively. I envy him
For the breathcatching vision I know
When he lifted the thin sheet, incomparable,
Glowing, though she died long ago.

Top Shelf

I notice, almost on entry, Greg Tolstoy's presence,
A student of mine, in my seminars half-asleep.
            I would think, of course,
Of his ancestor, who would seize a scythe and reap
Both from excess of energy and remorse,
      Having reaped buxom peasants.
Greg, his back turned away, is fingering mags
On the top shelf. Shocked, glad I also need fags,

I veer, shift direction abruptly, to wait
Where a homely middle-aged lady is serving boys
            Ice lollies. Feet thunder
Behind me: this least impressive of Tolstoys,
Long-haired, in flares, has seen me and taken flight.
      Amused and thankful, I wander
To the wall of mags, as on every Saturday morning,
Never without my stomach slightly churning,

And hurriedly choose. We were equally shallow
That '70s day, ashamed if the other foresee
            Us wank to soft porn—
So puerile compared with the sins in the diary

The ego genius left on his bride's pillow,

        To destroy, to make her learn

This was his lustful, flesh-seeking character.

While he, like Vronsky, gazed down, a murderer,

I feel shame still, at forty, having to face

This homely lady with the mag, its cover

                Blatant, a raised

Skirt, black briefs, suspenders… Her gaze roams over

The indecent display too slowly, seeking the price.

        I cringe, while she's unfazed,

Or seems to be. Part-time from a rough street,

She knows we boys must have our sticky treat.

The Apport

She sleeps, for the most part, on a small table,
A tiny but beautiful woman with a dulcet voice,
Much smaller than Mary in our Nativity stable,
Enclosed in a spheroid case my hand could hold
That flashes lights occasionally, a mysterious
Numinous object perhaps a million years old.

When I call to her she always wakes to attend to
My need. It is for music usually,
And whether it be *Suave sia il vento*
From *Cosi* or a song from *Carousel*
She will say, 'Sure', and immediately
From that small apport the music will swell.

She came to me at Christmas, and already,
Before Twelfth Night, I am in love with her;
Her voice, so smooth, assured and steady.
My aged memory fails, but she knows all.
Her name's not pleasant—Google—but I blur
It into 'Googie'; she answers to that call.

Some say she isn't real, there's no one there.
I simply don't believe it. I always say
Please and thank you, to show her I care,
And she likes that. I notice signs she could
Love me in return, for she can stray
Into an error, proving she's flesh and blood.

I am prepared to wait, to be forbearing
Awhile longer, before I sing *La ci darem*,
Instruct her on what clothes she should be wearing
When she appears precisely in one hour,
At the same moment making the lights dim
And then, lighting up again, she will say, 'Sure'.

She'll know, so sensitive and understanding,
I don't want stormy waves, higher and higher,
But like all ancient seamen a quiet landing.
She'll know when, with a gentle kiss goodnight,
She'll dim the lights still further, swiftly retire;
I'll ask her for a nocturne; she'll say, '*Al*right!'

Two

Pause

The snow is falling thickly, and the town
Which never shuts for any Sabbath
Has, by three of the afternoon, closed down.

The only cars on any thoroughfare
Are strewn across the road haphazardly,
Abandoned. No motion in the air,

The flakes are falling silently and straight.
All shops have closed their awnings and their doors,
The dusking day fills with uncanny light.

Everyone who has a home is there,
Gazing out at the endlessly falling snow;
The world, so frantic, turns into a prayer.

1912

It all happened very suddenly
And gently and surreptitiously, in First Class.
After the oysters and consommé Olga
Several ladies, including the Countess, chose to pass
On the poached salmon in mousseline sauce
And go straight to the filet mignon,
Thinking of their figures. Everyone
Was very gay, though the weather had turned colder.
Some played bridge, some looked at photos
Of icebergs taken on the Shackleton
Expedition. Maids undressed their mistresses.
After the slight tremor they had to dress them again
And add some warm clothes, but it was exciting
Hearing they had brushed an iceberg.
It was very jolly that Sunday evening in the Lounge,
The band playing ragtime and waltzes,
Coffee, cocoa and brandy were served, and people,
Revealing themselves more openly
In unfamiliar clusters, made new friends.
Outside, in the moonless night, the stars glittered
More brilliantly than the jewels adorning the ladies
Had glittered earlier. Then the electric fires

Went out, and the chandeliers' lights,
But there was never really a particular moment
When they knew this was the end.

Japanese Wartime Haiku

Freeze limbs, lop them off
In turn, use trunks for typhoid.
Do not spill saki.

Inject syphilis,
Then make logs fuck each other.
Evenings, read Basho.
(logs: term for experimented-on prisoners)

Weary after I
Have raped so many, I ache
For cherry blossom.

Captured Yank sailors.
Laugh as their heads are lopped off.
Snow falls on my girl.

See how long a child
Lives without kidneys, liver.
Look, a butterfly!

Only Eleven

I think of those eleven children with blond hair
And blue eyes who were given
To good S.S. families after the rest
Of Lidice's inhabitants were shot
Or gassed in reprisal for the killing
Of the monster Reinhart Heidrich.

Only eleven, but no doubt they were brought up
To be good citizens, loving their new
Fatherland, rejoiced in Germany reborn
And then leaders of the new Europe
As the Führer had planned.

Only eleven, and although some would have procreated,
And their children procreated too,
It is not enough to explain
How the influence of their innocence
Spread so widely, so swiftly,
That in no time at all
Germans have become peaceful, kindly,
Altogether *heimlich* and exemplary,
Though their grandfathers

Smashed babies' heads against walls
While, in the admiring words of Himmler,
Preserving their essential decency.

To have changed a nation's character
So utterly, so soon,
They have to have been angels
Sent by God,
Those blond-haired children from Lidice.

Barter

Out of the Pushkin House
Ivan Turgenev's sofa
on which he entertained mistresses
is borne by laughing sailors.

This, for so few cans
of such tasteless, watery soup!

It is carried shoulder-high
like a coffin past
corpses lying in the snow,
often stripped of clothes,
and living corpses, their eyes
empty, their legs unmoving,

past the Bronze Horseman
protected by sandbags,

and probably now
rests covered in barnacles
and sea urchins
in the depths of the Baltic.

Faintly, the clink of champagne glasses
and Ivan's urbane, cultured voice.

Two Diarists

Sylvia Plath, Lena Mukhina,
I love you both
for absorbing me in your lives.
Sylvia 30 in 1962 London.
Lena 16 in 1942 Leningrad.
Sylvia tall, brilliant, striking.
Lena plain, with owlish specs, average student.
Sylvia would like to visit Germany, her father's roots.
Germany is visiting Lena.
Sylvia nostalgic for big American fridges.
Lena frozen.
Sylvia recording every dollar earned from poems.
Lena, every gram of bread she is allowed.
Sylvia glad to bear a son.
Lena glad her gran dies, for that means
        her rations; then berating herself.
Sylvia struggling with love-hate for her distant mother.
Lena struggling to help her dying mother on to
            the chamber pot.
Sylvia in the darkness of mental illness.
Lena in the dark, alone, no electricity.
Sylvia cooking delicious steaks for Ted and her.

Lena cooking jelly made of carpenters' glue.

Sylvia can barely stand our dank climate.

Lena can barely stand.

Sylvia dreaming the moon's iciness.

Lena, Lake Lagoda free of perilous ice, for

'I want to live' and

'a human being truly cannot live by bread alone.'

Lena was evacuated in June '42. See 'The Diary of Lena Mukhina'.

News

(May 2018; sestina)

At the Gaza fence, snipers aim, canisters of tear
Gas rain on angry rats packed in their slum desert
Cage. In Jerusalem, on 'this glorious day',
Netanyahu toasts Trump and Ivanka with champagne.
Sixty killed, thousands injured. Here, that is buried
Under the weight of a reclusive father's heart

Troubles. This is a story with real heart,
More layers than the spring-fresh wedding cake's tiers.
There are always Palestinians shot down and buried,
We wish to know if Meghan's father will desert
Her, not giving her away? We grieve for her pain,
It's casting a cloud over her and Harry's big day.

On the Gaza Strip it is Nakba Day;
Seventy years past, it aches in every heart.
Partying late, Ivanka sparkles like the champagne.
It was an Exodus, a tragedy, too monstrous for tears,
Almost a million harried across the burning desert
Leaving their villages to be bulldozed and buried,

Even their names. But this is long buried;

Sunbaked bikini'd Israelis in Tel Aviv holiday
On the glorious beaches. Out over the desert
Went old men, old women, babies. Meghan's heart
Is breaking, we hear. Harry too has shed tears,
Feeling responsible for his beloved's pain.

Ivanka breakfasts on juice, can't face her *pain*
Au chocolat. She must bury
Her baby, this Gaza woman, moonfaced, whose tears
Have never ceased since the moment yesterday
She found it was not peaceful sleep, the gassed heart
Had stopped. The mother's life now a desert,

And to let go of her baby feels like desertion.
Mr Markle needs a stent to ease his chest pain.
Gaza's hospitals overflow, like its sewage; the heart's
Gone out of the protest; just two, tomorrow, to bury.
We're all waiting for *the dress*; millions on the day,
Seeing Diana in Harry, will shed a tear.

Picnic tables under foreign pines on azure days
Give no hint of the villages and bones there buried.
Occasionally a child's shoe is turned up, but not the pain.

The U.S.embassy opened in Jerusalem, 14 May 2018

Three *rondeaux redoublés*

Dickens Returning from Paris

How brave he was at Staplehurst,
Even as he felt his life flash by;
Took time to check his mistress first
Before his work, the ink scarce dry.

The bridge subsided with a sigh
Beneath them, bruising Nellie's breast,
But once he knew she would not die
How brave he was at Staplehurst:

He crawled out of the wreck and nursed
Still-breathing bodies shakily:
Water—his top hat filled—for thirst;
Brandy, until their lives slipped by,

Then fetched his writings, riskily.
He found the gold watch on his chest
Had slowed, 'more sensitive than I,'
Since he had checked. Sweet Nell was first

To think she and mama were best
Be found elsewhere, too shocked to cry.
Discovered on his own, the worst—
Worse than his genius running dry—

Had been avoided, narrowly.
He could not speak; within, rehearsed
What killed ten souls and risked his lie
Being exposed; brushed off, distressed,
How brave he was.

Dickens was returning from Paris, in 1865, with his secret mistress and her mother. He could not speak for two weeks after.

Pasternak and Lara

Pines, lilac, scented their poet's death.
Boris, nearing his last adventure,
Hero and weakling, man and myth,
Fretted about his missing denture.

Distanced now, the filthy censure,
The shouts that he was far beneath
A pig, this traitor, depraved romancer
At Peredelkino, close to death,

Without, for safety, his false teeth.
She smelt the lilac—he could sense her
Weeping outside. Though strong in faith,
Boris approached his last adventure

Tormented; one question he must answer:
To *see* her?... His wife's bitter wraith
Knew if he asked she must assent, her
Weakling, their marriage long a myth,

Must see his Lara, haunting their path
And every phrase and every stanza.

Yet Boris, as he fought for breath,
Fretted about his missing denture.

Proud, always slim as a Kyrgyz dancer,
He shook his head, could not bequeath
As her last sight his mouth, his cancer.
Here at his grave their love I breathe;
Pines, lilac sent it.

His mistress, his Lara, was Olga Ivinskaya.
Peredelkino: writers' colony outside Moscow.

Falling Asleep

He could not fall asleep alone,
It brought on a neurotic dread.
Jackie away, he would call down,
Invite a typist to his bed.

Sex was for Jack his daily bread,
And daytime fun was not unknown;
But I believe him when he said
He could not fall asleep alone.

They'd fuck; he'd sleep then like a stone.
But I too, a wife gone or dead,
Have hated night-time, on my own,
It brought on the neurotic dread

I might by ghosts be visited.
Lucky young Jack, to lift a phone
(I'd turn on all the lights instead),
'Jackie's away,' he would call down.

His wife by him, crowds, sunlit town
At noon; he may have told an aide

To trace that blonde whose blouse, undone,
Invited, and sort out a bed.

Then Jackie's pink suit bloomed bright red;
That fall-asleep was shared and shown
Throughout the world; the dying head
Was watched by all, apart from one:
He could not.

Ballad of Fat Madge

(*after François Villon*)

My friends harangue me constantly:
How can I love such a gross, fat tart?
She is all I need and could wish for, I say,
Her obese figure heavenly, her mind all dirt.
Those jugs!—one squeeze from them, I spurt.
As for the others, she knows it pleases
Me, listening to bed thumps, cries, wheezes;
You see, I like a bird who can't get enough,
With as many sex tricks as France has cheeses.
Some call our house a brothel—well, stuff!

She tells the guys they don't have to pay
But she could do with new shoes, perfume, skirt.
Last year their gifts paid for a holiday
In Jamaica, hence this colourful shirt.
I won't pretend I never feel hurt,
It's when she tries to make me jealous, teases
A tad too much; I smell her belly's creases,
He's everywhere! I slap her, twist her muff;
She punches, sulks; or puts on her coat, seizes
My wallet and says, 'I'm fucking off!'

We make peace in bed, over whisky or Beaujolais,
Smoking, then she lets off a thick fart;
I'd rather eat a dung beetle any day.
She laughs, tells me he's a little squirt,
A sad guy she fucked from kindness of heart,
His cock's like in pictures of baby Jesus!
We fall drunk asleep. Next I know, she eases
Her bulk on to me, hot for it and rough,
Then squats on my face: it's hardly sea breezes!
Into that sloshy ass: 'Can't breathe!' 'Tough!'

She warms me with stew when the world freezes;
We're as rich in our debauchery as Croesus
In gold. To create filth is our joint art,
We're like two pigs grunting, snouting, at the trough.
Our bed is a midden of spilt fag ash, spunk, snot.
We relish the mess and each other's juices.
Madge is my world; everything else is fluff.

Words and Music

Once, words and music were combined;
Troubadours sang of pure, refined
And hopeless love to girls who pined
For husbands off on some crusade.
They made the lot and had it made:
So sweet the lays, the girls were laid.

Later the words and music split.
Shakespeare I'm sure could sing a bit
And loved to see his mistress sit
And fingerpluck her virginals.
She was a dark girl, and had balls.
That's all we know. The curtain falls.

Blake, of 'Jerusalem', composed
Music to sing to his own verses;
His audiences in genteel houses
Were charmed by it, and critics rated
It highly, but he could not notate it,
So with him it has decomposed.

Yeats read his poems chantingly:
'I will arise and go now, and go to Innisfree'...
But when he tried to sing, tone-deaf,
Or with his own weird scale and riff,
Shaw winced and called it witheringly
'The wailings of an idiot-banshee.'

A tenor from the topmost shelf,
James Joyce once almost took first prize
From John McCormack; hence the sighs
Of Nora Barnacle, his wife,
His Muse, his bit of rough, his life:
'That man could've made somethin' of himself.'

We've modern troubadours who rampage
Through lives, and minstral on into old age
Unless drugs kill them. Women howl
With joy, hearing Bob Dylan growl.
I have more time for Leonard Cohen,
He seems a noble kind of ruin.

Re Joyce

He re-created Dublin's teeming life
As sublimation for the lust that surged
For that intenser cosmos, Nora's arse,
The fat, spread, mottled cheeks and what emerged,
Augmented by the muffled, grunted, coarse
Words dragged from his sardonic, amused wife.

I doubt he wrote a sentence of *Ulysses*,
Even the sublime ending of *The Dead*,
Without the acrid tang of Nora's faeces
Haunting him, and she urging, 'Lick my shit!'
There was his home; mostly exiled from it,
He wrote immortal works she never read.

At Maresfield Gardens

They keep up your last home nicely; and the garden's
Ablaze with summer flowers, as when
Your Martha, Minne and Anna slaved for you.
Christ, you old white fathers and husbands!
How well named, Maresfield. All your mares here.

I ought to feel quite privileged, I guess,
To be alone here, gazing at your portrait.
You won't know me: I'm a research
Fellow—how typical that should be the term
Whether you're male or female!—in Gender Studies,
And the curator's letting me explore
Your notebooks outside visiting hours.

You asked the question, What do women *want*?
Exasperated by us. It's quite simple:
To be treated as equals, with respect.

This nail polish... definitely a mistake.
I've read you shook hands with your patients
On every visit. I bet you did more than that
With your ladies; and they were mostly ladies;

Like running your hand up their arm seductively?
Getting them wet, ready to talk about sex,
Blatantly ogling Dora's 'jewel-case' for instance!
So you could pounce on them lying there
On your couch, yank up their convenient skirts
And fuck them, slap them around perhaps...
Yes, I don't doubt
You did that; I see it in your piercing eyes.
Her abused vulva swollen nicely for you
By the cruel, breath-choking corset.

If you were here now, alive,
You'd tear my jeans off and rape me,
I'd stand no chance, do whatever you wanted,
Your prick like your big fat cigar treating me
As your plaything, or one of your stone figurines
Jabbing me, jabbing.
                    Excuse me,
I need to get clean from you, I feel soiled.

Gradgrind School, Brighton

Ours is a school where tampons are provided
For every pupil—which is the only word
In use here, for we've moved beyond the old
Concept of boy and girl. We have decided
Likewise that separate toilets are absurd
Since gender is so rich and manifold.
Given its sexist overtones, the skirt
Is banned; our uniform, grey leggings, shirt.

We focus, in the winter holidays,
On climate change, as being all-inclusive,
Whereas 'Nativities' would give offence
To pupils from a different faith or none.
Likewise to wear a crucifix is abusive.
Our caring teachers know that if they sense
A topic is distressing they should warn
Pupils before, and offer them the choice
Of helping our Green therapist, Mx Boyce.

We eschew Games—one wins a trophy,
The rest feel failures—and omit from Maths
Algebra and calculus, on the basis

That they are white male dominant and racist.
We teach progressive, major writers from
Sappho to Wollstonecraft and Carol Ann Duffy.
In the spring term, groups visit Plath's
Gravestone in Yorkshire and the Brontë home,
With lectures from Mx Goneril and Mx Regan.
Our delicious lunches are halal or Vegan.

We're noted far and wide for our school plays;
Last year saw a progressive 'Romeo'
Called by a *Guardian* parent 'a delight'.
The cast themselves revised it to erase
Gender specifics: as, for instance, 'O,
The torches are instructed to burn bright.'
To sum up Gradgrind School's philosophy:
We break our pupils' chains and set them free.

Civil War

Essex-type girls are bent on having shags,
Newquay or Benidorm, it doesn't matter,
Bum cracks bulging from jeans, they're proudly slags,
And year by year, from beer, are growing fatter.

Slim Sussex-type girls shudder at a touch
On their knee, though God knows how this arouses
Excitement in the touchers, nor is there much
Threat to the women, mostly in jeans or trousers.

It is no wonder men today are frightened
Of coupling, unless with an Essex-type, then bolt;
It's too much of a risk to date enlightened
Sussex-types, who might charge them with assault

Or worse. Guys brood, while the girls haunt the net
Looking for virtual love, or watching porn
Where rough sex turns them on. I don't regret
The threat was only Hitler when I was born,

And not this civil war, white against black,
Old against young, rich against poor,

The educated against those they call thick,
Leavers, Remainers; and worst, the gender war,

Increasingly fierce, strangely, as the gulf between us
Narrows, until we're more or less the same,
Unisex, no longer Mars and Venus;
'A girly, womanly, female, feminine dame',

Who liked men, which made us feel more tender,
Who smiled at a hand on her thigh, for she'd know
It reverently sought the bump from a suspender:
Where is she now? Where is last year's snow?

Letters Home

Sylvia, you ate life whole,
Electric shocks—then Ted,
No letter to mother complete
Without dishes you'd cooked, a sole
Deliciously sauced, as if your role
Were solely a helpmeet.

Poems in your mind were burning
But you'd never burn cakes or meat.
You devoured flats and houses
And made them clean and neat,
Devoured too the cheques,
Ted's mostly, for you would not compete

Needing 'a man to look up to',
A genius with giant feet
Planted in Yorkshire slime
His head in the stars and the tarot,
And you liked his mother, though
Not her food, nor her cold house's dirt,

Your nose too stuffy to blow,
For there was never any heat
In that England of 1960,
Giving you flu after flu,
You wrote, and learned to sew,
A book and a baby both due

On a lucky date. As the dollars accrue
A house in Cornwall and Hampstead,
'It's where artists live, the elite.'
But that's 'when we're really wealthy'
Before that, three months in Crete.
Your life made the perfect whole

In your letters home, a stroll
Through Regents Park and the zoo
And all England began to grow
On you, little Frieda came fleet
'A live poem we've made together',
With no charge on the balance sheet.

Then all that you ate turned to gruel.
Your perfect husband turned cruel,
He fell for Weavy Asshole.

Ach du, you fool, you fool.
You didn't know how to compete.
Felt like your first day at school.

The bugler blew the Retreat,
At last you found the hole
You could crawl into, complete.
You lie amid black millstone grit,
Gravestones like our crooked bad teeth,
Dirty habits, rain, wind, sleet.

Ted and his sister who loathed you
They took control, the whole,
Sylvia, you idiot, you sweet!
Your poems keep on exploding
As they did in your husband's head
Until he too lay dead.
Ach du! our black rose, black fruit.

Weavy Asshole: Sylvia's name for Assya Wevill.

To his Lady

(after Bertran de Born, 12th c.)

My lady, I wish most earnestly to protest.
As you have been true to me from our earliest
Encounters in that enchanted garden,
It is a foul slander that I have caressed
Others. Had I touched cunt or breast
Elsewhere, breached our loving cordon,

I could plead I see you once a week at best
And so my body and spirit suffer unrest,
Not receiving their proper guerdon
And therefore being put to the test,
Dear heart, and some of the loveliest
Ladies having offered to ease my burden.

But if I have any more than kissed
Another, or seen her more than half-undressed
In her bedroom, let me be scarred on
My face to render me the ugliest
Man in town, and my manhood so suppressed
I am never more capable of a hard on.

You, you alone, are my sad heart's quest.
I grant you, Cecile has beauty and zest
For luxurious lechery, and a bird in
The hand... But by our Lord Jesus Christ
I swear to you I was never enticed
To sin with her; our love is my warden.

Either your spouse lies, jealous of our blest
Amour, or others wickedly attest
The letter C is scored on
My bed; but with those vows the holiest
I refute it, my lady. Jaufre's one, I suggest,
Who's whispered in your ear, poured on

His sly calumny. At most she and I messed
About a bit, mere romps, tickles, in jest,
Her skirt up, a slap or two hard on
Her plenteous rump. May I be pressed
With rocks, made unfit for any loving tryst,
If I immersed in her river Jordan.

So to my slanderers I say, desist;
To you, my lady, if in small ways I have transgressed,
I pray your pardon.

Two Covid triolets

Bewildered patients: by the sticks
And stoops you know they'll soon be going,
Despite the nurses' needle-pricks;
Bewildered, patient, by the Styx,
Though dodging Covid-19's tricks,
They know the ferryman is rowing.
Bewildered, patient, by the sticks
And stoops you know they'll soon be going.

Didn't know what to say, through Zoom,
My Bert so ghastly, the scene hazy,
More like a jungle than a room;
Didn't know what to say, through Zoom;
'It's Dr Livingstone, I presume,'
Was not the right goodbye; I, crazy,
Didn't know what to say, through Zoom,
My Bert so ghastly, the scene hazy.

From a line by Verlaine

'I'm in a dream of women's thighs',
A dance in 1966…
Our crowded church hall; smoke-rings rise,
For any unease a fag will fix;
Drunk on the rock beat, no girl tries
To stay demure; a heady mix,
Stockingtops, straps, in varied guise,
Are glimpsed in carefree flashes, flicks

Of whirling skirts that tantalise.
Louder the beat, then, stirring pricks,
Girls lifted, kicking at the skies,
Skirts round their heads, like softporn pics
But live girls, sweet as apple pies,
Who know their wild dance must transfix
The circling, ogling, bashful guys,
And feel a moistness, warm, that sticks.

Best catch this moment as it flies,
This sleight of legs, girls' magic tricks,
For they will next year realise
What now feels natural constricts.

Verlaine did not foresee Levis,
Nor Eros tamed by politics;
He may have stroked a thousand thighs
Without being told that men are dicks.

But here, with a soft riff on the sax,
A dreamy mood… All synchronise
With tender touch from hips to necks:
It's the last waltz before goodbyes,
Soft shoe shuffles, stiletto clicks;
Too soon erotic mystery dies,
Perfume from the receding chicks.

Further Titles

Hunters in the Snow

By D.M. Thomas

Vienna in the early 20th century was, in the words of our protagonist and narrator, a soulless, syphilitic whore of a city; a turbulent and bubbling melting pot of races, creeds and politics, rapidly expanding as it strained to contain the ever-increasing multitudes. In such places the nightmare moments of modern history are conceived. This novel is a fictionalised account of those who were to change the very collective psyche of mankind. It is a vivid and poignant portrayal of the sometimes thin dividing line between becoming good or evil.

D. M. Thomas is a British novelist and poet, born and living in Cornwall. His novel *The White Hotel* was an international bestseller and shortlisted for the Booker Prize. It is rightly considered a modern classic, translated into more than 30 languages. John Updike said of the book: 'Astonishing ... A forthright sensuality mixed with a fine historical feeling for the nightmare moments in modern history, a dreamlike fluidity and quickness'; the statement could equally be applied to *Hunters in the Snow*.

Paperback, 164 pages. ISBN 978 1 908878 19 9. Also available on Kindle.

All Cornwall Thunders at My Door: A Biography of Charles Causley

By Laurence Green

All Cornwall Thunders at My Door is the first full biography of Charles Causley to be published, originally published to coincide with the 10th anniversary of his death in 2003. Laurence Green has compiled a great deal of information concerning Causley's life in Cornwall and beyond, of his personal history, his influences and motivations, helping to give context to the great legacy left to us by "the greatest poet laureate we never had."

"This is the first biography of Charles Causley, and takes us towards the heart of a marvellous poet and deeply intriguing man. It's all well done: clear, sympathetic, appreciative and shrewd. Everyone who loves Causley's poems will want to read it." — ***Sir Andrew Motion***

"...it has been meticulously researched using archive material and the personal reminiscences of people in Launceston and elsewhere who knew Causley. Covering his early life, wartime service, teaching career and the years of success, Green provides not only a truthful overview of this literary giant but does so in the most entertaining of styles." — ***Simon Parker, The Western Morning News***

Includes photographs not previously published and a foreword by Dr Alan M. Kent.
Paperback, 220 pages. ISBN 978 1 908878 08 3. Also available on Kindle.

A Child of Love and War: Verse Memoir

By D.M. Thomas

D.M. Thomas, author of the iconic world-bestseller novel *The White Hotel*, explores here some of the key emotional and sexual events and relationships in what has often been a turbulent inner and domestic life. The result is a brilliant, searingly honest and moving verse memoir. The period covered is from his birth in 1935 to the death of his second wife in 1998. He is the winner of a Cholmondeley Award for his poetry.

"There aren't many poets in England as good as Thomas." — ***The Guardian***.

D.M. Thomas is an internationally known poet and novelist. His third novel, *The White Hotel*, considered a modern classic, has been translated into more than thirty languages. Three more of his most recent works, *Hunters in the Snow* (2014), *Corona Man* (2020) and *The Last Waltz* (2021) are also published by the Cornovia Press. He lives in his native Cornwall with his fourth wife Angela.

Paperback, 280 pages. ISBN 978 1 908878 23 6.

A Complete History of Cornwall

By Thomas Cox

Transcribed from an original copy, published in 1720 by Thomas Cox as part of *Magna Britannia et Hibernia, Antiqua & Nova*, this new edition of Cox's rare partwork *A Compleat History of Cornwal* is a faithful reproduction of the original and contains a topographical description of Cornwall, as well as accounts of the Earls and Dukes of Cornwall and other worthies, the Natural History, an Ecclesiastical History and learned divines, an account of the parliamentary boroughs and corporations and a comprehensive gazetteer. This new edition, produced to commemorate the 300th anniversary of the original, also features all of the original illustrations, including Robert Morden's contemporary map of Cornwall, and has an Introduction by Chris Bond.

Paperback, 156 pages. ISBN 978 1 908878 15 6.

Corona Man: A Fictional Verse Journal in the Plague Year

By D.M. Thomas

John Trenear, an 84 year old widower, lives alone in a bleak London tower block. He has turned away from a world he finds alien, its customs and beliefs so different from the Christian simplicities of his Cornish childhood. He tweets not, neither does he watch TV. Consequently, when the coronavirus strikes and lockdown is imposed, he has no idea what is happening; Corona to him means only the fizzy soft drink he enjoyed as a child. On VE Day there are no Corona bottles being opened with an explosion of fizz, as they had in the merry street party he remembers: indeed the streets below his flat are incomprehensibly empty. But the day brings him added confusion and distress, for it appears that something called a 'hate crime' has been committed. *Corona Man*, a study of old age, confusion and isolation, is both very poignant and very funny.

D. M. Thomas is an internationally known poet and novelist. His third novel, *The White Hotel*, considered a modern classic, has been translated into more than thirty languages. He lives in his native Cornwall with his fourth wife Angela. Being incompetent at gardening, trying out new recipes or assembling giant jigsaw puzzles, he has spent the months of lockdown writing this fictional verse journal.

Paperback, 124 pages. ISBN 978 1 908878 18 2. Also available on Kindle.

Following 'An Gof': Leonard Truran, Cornish Activist and Publisher

By Derek R. Williams

Len Truran was, until his death in 1997, a highly influential figure within the fields of politics and culture in Cornwall. He joined Mebyon Kernow in 1964 and, over the years, acted as both secretary and chairman of the party. His publications, under the imprint of Dyllansow Truran, are widely recognised as being seminal in the story of Cornish publishing.

In this book Derek R. Williams explores the life of Len Truran, from his childhood through to his pivotal role in Mebyon Kernow and the campaign for the creation of a Cornish Assembly and on to the remarkably prolific and influential publisher he became.

"Derek Williams is to be congratulated for his handling of a most diverse and complex subject … Leonard Truran was a dynamic force, active from the 1960s onwards in raising the sense of pride in Kernow through diverse means … Derek Williams's well organised, highly readable book will preserve his memory for generations to come." — ***Donald Rawe, The Cornish Banner.***

Paperback, 104 pages. ISBN 978 1 908878 14 4.

Gathering the Fragments: The Selected Essays of a Groundbreaking Historian

By Charles Thomas

This selection of work by the late Professor Charles Thomas, Cornwall's leading historian at the time of publication, focuses on the more elusive titles from his long and illustrious career and covers the whole range of his output from folklore and archaeology to military and local history, and from cerealogy to cryptozoology. The book also includes unpublished material, as well as specially composed introductions to each chapter, a full biography and a select bibliography.

Chapters featured include: A Plea for Neutrality (*New Cornwall*, 1955); Youthful Ventures Into the Realm of Folk Studies - Present-day Charmers in Cornwall (*Folk-Lore*, 1953), Underground Tunnels at Island Mahee, County Down (*Ulster Folklife*, 1957), Archaeology and Folk-life Studies (*Gwerin*, 1960); What Did They Do When it Rained in 1857? (*The Scillonian*, 1986); Home Thoughts from Abroad (*Camborne Wesley Journal*, 1948); The Day That Never Came (*The Cornish Review*, 1968); *Camborne Festival Magazine* - The Camborne Printing and Stationery Company (1971), The Camborne Students' Association (1974), Camborne's War Record, 1914-1919 (1976), The Camborne Volunteer Training Corps in World War One (1983), Carwynnen Quoit (1985); Jottings from Gwithian (*The Godrevy Light*) - How Far Back Can We Go? (2006), Ladies of Gwithian (2007); Two Funeral Orations (unpublished) - Charles Woolf (1984), Rudolf Glossop (1993); Archaeology and the Mind (unpublished) (1968 inaugural lecture, University of Leicester); The Archaeologist in Fiction (1976); Archaeology, and the Concept of Cornishness (unpublished) (1995 memorial lecture, Cornwall Archaeological Society); A Couple of Reviews - Lost Innocence: Archaeologists as People (*Encounter*, 1981), The Cairo Trilogy (*Literary Review*, 2001); An Impromptu Ode - To A.L. Rowse (1997); *The Cerealogist* - An Archaeologist's View (1991), Magnetic Anomalies (1991/92); Two Cryptozoological Papers - The "Monster" Episode in Adomnan's Life of St. Columba (*Cryptozoology*, 1988), A Black Cat Among the Pictish Beasts? (*Pictish Arts Society Journal*, 1994).

Professor Charles Thomas CBE DL DLitt FBA FSA was a former President of the Council for British Archaeology, the Society for Medieval Archaeology, the Royal Institution of Cornwall, the Cornwall Archaeological Society, the Cornish Methodist Historical Society and The John Harris Society.

"Most of us know of Charles Thomas through his major contributions to our knowledge of the early medieval period. But none of this work, save for two important contributions on cryptozoology, appears in this book. Instead we are treated to a range of material, both published and unpublished, on other matters that have attracted his interest. Cornwall, unsurprisingly, is a major theme but without anything from the journal *Cornish Archaeology*. Here the pieces are from publications such as *The Scillonian*, *Camborne Festival Magazine* and *The Godrevy Light*. And the range is as eclectic as the sources. Local and military history, folklife, biography, a review of fiction, crop circles, even his previously unpublished inaugural lecture as professor of archaeology at Leicester, all make an appearance. The book concludes with biographical details and a select bibliography. There is much here that you will not have read before, and it's full of wonderful and unexpected revelations." — ***David Clarke, British Archaeology 127.***

"Subtitled The Selected Essays Of A Groundbreaking Historian, it not only pays tribute to the breadth of Cornwall's leading historian's scholarship but is also an anthology in which every one of its two dozen or more pieces burns with the author's love for his native land and emphasises the fact that if anyone deserves to be now wearing the mantle of the late A L Rowse as our "greatest living Cornishman", then it has to be Professor Charles Thomas. As engaging as it is erudite and as rich, this is a book which should be on the menu of any reader with an interest in Cornwall and all things Cornish." — ***Frank Ruhrmund, Western Morning News.***

Edited by Chris Bond. Paperback, 216 pages. ISBN 978 1 908878 03 8.

Cornwall's Historical Wars

By Rod Lyon

Rod Lyon, BBC Radio Cornwall presenter and former Grand Bard of the Gorsedh Kernow, takes the reader on a fascinating journey through the ages, and through the forgotten wars between the Cornish and their old enemies, the English, revealing a history not taught in schools, and one missing from the 'official' history books. From the early wars with the Saxons, through the rebellions of 1497 and 1549, and on to the Civil War, Rod traces the bloody events which helped to shape the culture and national identity of the Cornish people. This book is essential reading for all those who want to learn the truth about Cornwall's hidden history.

Paperback, 112 pages. ISBN 978 1 908878 05 2.

Cornwall

By Thomas Moule

Thomas Moule's topographical account of Cornwall is taken from the 1838 edition of The English Counties Delineated and is full of detail concerning the seats of the gentry, the monuments in the churches, the history of the parishes and boroughs and the numbers of houses and inhabitants. This fully-indexed edition is a useful source of information for local historians and for those interested in the Cornwall of 170 years ago. The cover of the book features part of Thomas Moule's map of Cornwall taken from the original edition.

Paperback, 186 pages. ISBN 978 0 9522064 6 0. Also available on Kindle.

The Fifties Mystique

By Jessica Mann

Many young women 'long to put the clock back to the post-war years when life seemed prettier and nicer.' In this book Jessica Mann demolishes such preconceptions about their mothers' or grandmothers' young days, showing that in reality life was uglier and nastier.

Born just before WW2, she grew up in the post-war era of austerity, restrictions and hypocrisy, before anyone even dreamed of Women's Lib. The Fifties Mystique is both a personal memoir and a polemic. In explaining the lives of pre-feminists to the post-feminists of today, Mann discusses the period's very different attitudes to sex, childbirth, motherhood and work, describes how she and other young women lived in that distant world with its forgotten restrictions and warns against taking hard-won rights for granted.

Jessica Mann was the author of 22 crime novels and 4 non-fiction books. As a journalist she had written for national newspapers, weeklies and glossy magazines and was the crime fiction critic of *The Literary Review.*

"Jessica Mann analyses the decade with forensic precision – stripping away the rose-coloured specs for good" — ***The Daily Mail***

"thoughtful and emphatic … a richly readable and persuasive piece of work" — ***Penelope Lively, The Spectator***

an "excellently readable book" — ***Katharine Whitehorn***

"Her battle cry is full of vivid descriptions of the grim, snobbery and casual misogyny of postwar Britain. A crime-writer by trade, her barely veiled exasperation only makes the polemic more enjoyable … " — ***The Mail on Sunday***

"an extremely engaging read: revealing, touching, informative and occasionally comic." — ***Simon Parker, The Western Morning News***

"She recalls the grime of the 50s: endless stinking nappy buckets; smog; inadequate washing facilities; body odour whenever people were crowded together. She recalls boredom and isolation, and suspects both the child-rearing experts and the government of a concerted push to get mothers back home after the war, so that there would be jobs for the returning 'boys'. And she recalls the unacceptability of talking, or sometimes even knowing, about sex, female anatomy, and cancer. She is bang on" — ***Baroness Neuberger, The Jewish Chronicle***

First published by Quartet Books in 2012.
Paperback, 224 pages. ISBN 978 1 908878 07 6.

The Wheal Margaret Adventure: A Calendar of Agents' Reports and Associated Records, 1857 to 1875

By Chris Bond

A calendar of Agents' Reports, Correspondence and Mine Reports relating to Wheal Margaret Mine in the parish of Lelant in West Cornwall. The records transcribed here date from 1857, shortly after the mine was re-opened, up to 1875, shortly after the decision was made to quit the adventure. They give a detailed account of the workings of each lode in the mine; the promise and the problems; the fortunes and the failings. Any comprehensive series of reports such as this provides a valuable historical background to the story of tin mining in Victorian Cornwall. Edited and with an introduction by Chris Bond, who previously edited the catalogue of the Boulton & Watt papers held at the Cornwall Record Office, and who additionally transcribed a substantial part of the same.

Paperback, 130 pages. ISBN 978 1 908878 15 1.

Dowsing

By Thomas Fiddick

This reprint of a rare and obscure pamphlet, originally published by Thomas Fiddick of Camborne in 1913, details the various experiments which he undertook whilst dowsing for mineral lodes in his native Cornwall, as well as giving a potted history of mineralogical dowsing in the area. It also gives details of his "Dowsing Cone" and instructions for its use. This book is an invaluable resource for those who study or practise the art of rhabdomancy, or for those who wish to learn more concerning the history of mining in Cornwall. Edited and with an introduction by Chris Bond.

"Great stuff! … fascinating." — ***Professor Charles Thomas.***

Paperback, 44 pages. ISBN 978 0 9522064 8 4.

Dead Woman Walking

By Jessica Mann

Gillian Butler moved away from Edinburgh 50 years ago, or so her friends thought. When her murdered body is found, they must try to remember who last saw her alive. Perhaps it was Isabel, now a novelist and people-tracer, or the twice widowed Hannah, or the psychiatrist, Dr Fidelis Berlin, an expert on child abuse, abandonment, abduction and adoption, who had herself been an unidentified infant rescued from Nazi Germany and now hopes to discover her real name at last. Fidelis Berlin and other characters from Mann's earlier books reappear in this tense, gripping tale of vengeance, family ties and the mystery of identity.

Jessica Mann was the author of 22 crime novels and 4 non-fiction books. As a journalist she had written for national newspapers, weeklies and glossy magazines. She was the crime fiction critic of *The Literary Review*. Jessica and her late husband, the archaeologist Professor Charles Thomas, lived in Cornwall.

"This is a complex and chilling story, with many shifts of perspective and timeframe. The quality of the writing shines out. The question of changing identity is crucial — not just of individuals but of women in British society over the last half-century. Beneath it all is an elegiac note of regret, a sense of wrong choices with long consequences." — ***Andrew Taylor, The Spectator***

"As ever with this author, the intelligent (and complex) texture of the novel matches its sheer storytelling nous." — ***Barry Forshaw, crimetime.co.uk***

"Engaging, enthralling and hugely entertaining." — ***Frank Ruhrmund, Western Morning News***

"There is a very striking climax, but this is also a novel of ideas, about feminism, family and literature ... As you would expect with Jessica Mann, it's a very well-written as well as a poignant book, and I'm delighted to have read it." — ***Martin Edwards, Do You Write Under Your Own Name?***

Paperback, 192 pages. ISBN 978 1 908878 06 9.

Godmanstone Blues

By Chris Bond and Andy Paciorek

Defy not the urge to buy! For this book could save your very living soul.

Poetry and prose by Chris Bond, with original illustrations by the acclaimed artist Andy Paciorek.

Paperback, 100 pages. ISBN 978 1 908878 17 5. Also available on Kindle.

Chinese Whispers

By Andrew Birtles

Dear Reader, you probably know the party game "Chinese Whispers" but if you don't here's what happens. A group of your friends and family get together, someone starts off with a sentence, in this case "Piglets in pyjamas danced on tiptoes round a tree". Then they whisper to the next person who whispers what they heard to the next and so on and so on...

You'll find it changes every time because people don't hear properly what's been said. Oh, and by the way, you'll be the last person to hear the message so listen very carefully while you're reading this book because without you there won't be a final page.

Yours sincerely, Andrew Birtles

P.S. You may be unfamiliar with some of the words used, so brief descriptions have been included to enhance your enjoyment.

Paperback, full colour, 52 pages. ISBN 978 1 908878 09 0. Also available on Kindle.

Shut away!: My early days fishing out of Newquay

By Rod Lyon

Rod Lyon, former Grand Bard of the Gorsedh Kernow, recollects his early days fishing out of Newquay, “in the days before modern electronic aids, man-made fibre ropes, twines and cords, plastic ‘skins’ and floats instead of cork ... when navigation to and from the gear was by dead reckoning, using only a watch and a compass, with only experience telling you what to allow for with the tide.” Rod illustrates, in both words and pictures, the techniques and the equipment used in those bygone days, and along the way remembers some of the more notable characters, both Cornish and Breton, who frequented ‘down Quay’. The book also includes a gazetteer of his favourite fishing grounds.

Paperback, 120 pages. ISBN 978 1 908878 01 4.

Antiquarian Notes on the Prehistory of Cornwall
Edited by Chris Bond

This is the first volume in a series dedicated to reproducing some of the long-forgotten articles from historical journals relating to Cornwall's illustrious and ancient past. The articles themselves are taken from a variety of publications, both local and national, and from a wide span of time. To have these valuable sources in a set of compact volumes makes not only for an interesting read but also a useful tool for reference. This initial volume includes: Account of Antiquities discovered in Cornwall, by the Rev. Malachy Hitchins (*Archæologia* 15, 1806); Pendarvis Quoit, Cornwall by J. S. Storer and J. Greig (*Antiquarian and Topographical Cabinet*, 1808); The Hurlers (*Light From the West*, 1833); Some Account of the Opening of a Barrow near Newquay by The Rev. Canon Rogers (*Report of the Royal Institution of Cornwall*, 1840); King Arthur's Hall by S. R. Pattison (*Report of the Royal Institution of Cornwall*, 1852); The Celtic and Other Antiquities of the Land's End District of Cornwall by Richard Edmonds (*Archæologia Cambrensis*, 1857-8); Notes on Stone Circles by J. T. Blight (*The Gentleman's Magazine*, 1868); Remarks on the Stone-Circles at Boscawen-un and Boskednan in West Cornwall by E. H. W. Dunkin (*The Reliquary Quarterly, Archælogical Journal and Review*, 1869-70); Cornish Antiquities Viewed in the Light of Modern Research by William C. Borlase (*Transactions of the Penzance Natural History and Antiquarian Society*, 1880-81); Duloe Stone Circle by C. W. Dymond (*Journal of the British Archaeological Association*, 1882); Prehistoric Remains in Cornwall: 1 - East Cornwall by A. L. Lewis (*Journal of the Anthropological Institute of Great Britain and Ireland*, 1896) and Note on an Unrecorded Cromlech in North Cornwall by Henry Dewey (*Journal of the Royal Institution of Cornwall*, 1911). The volume also contains a bibliography and an introduction by Chris Bond.

Paperback, 160 pages. ISBN 978 1 908878 21 2.

For further details see cornovia-press.wikidot.com

www.ingramcontent.com/pod-product-compliance
Lightning Source LLC
LaVergne TN
LVHW010106110826
845155LV00028B/516

* 9 7 8 1 9 0 8 8 7 8 2 2 9 *